A.S. KELSEY

BEGINNER'S PHOTOGRAPHY GUIDE

The Ultimate Guide to Learning How to Take Photos All the Time, Learn Expert Photography Tips and Pointers to Snap the Perfect Photo Each Time

Descrierea CIP a Bibliotecii Naţionale a României
A.S. KELSEY
   BEGINNER'S PHOTOGRAPHY GUIDE. The Ultimate
Guide to Learning How to Take Photos All the Time, Learn
Expert Photography Tips and Pointers to Snap the Perfect Photo
Each Time / A.S. Kelsey – Bucharest: Editura My Ebook, 2021
   ISBN

A.S. KELSEY

BEGINNER'S PHOTOGRAPHY GUIDE

The Ultimate Guide to Learning How to Take Photos All the Time, Learn Expert Photography Tips and Pointers to Snap the Perfect Photo Each Time

My Ebook Publishing House
Bucharest, 2021

100 PHOTOGRAPHY TIPS

1. Gather photography information as much as you can.

To begin with your career in photography at the right path, you need to gather more information about it first. Gathering information would provide you guidance on the right steps that you need to take. Researching can be done through the internet, talking to professional photographers, as well as reading some books about the subject.

2. Purchase the digital camera that you want.

Even if you are still at the starting point of your photography career, it is best to purchase the type of digital camera that you really want. You should purchase something that can provide you with the kind of pictures that you want. By using a camera that provides quality photos, you would become more motivated in taking more pictures with it, even if you are still trying to learn about it.

3. Invest in a tripod.

Having a tripod can provide you with lots of benefits, as far as taking pictures is concerned. It is one of the things that you need to invest on, in order to have quality landscape shots. Aside from that, it would also help you in taking glorious pictures of sunset or sunrise.

4. Time your shots well.

Timing your shots well is one of the keys in taking beautiful pictures. This is actually one of the reasons why some professional photographers would suggest beginners in the field, to make use of filmed cameras at the start. This is because, using such types of cameras can help a person develop a good habit in timing and choosing his shots, due to the fact that the film limits it.

5. Don't hesitate to try new angles.

There is always a tendency for a beginner to stick on taking pictures of his subject head on. If you are doing that, you may be preventing yourself in finding the best angles. Thus, it is a good idea to try out different angles first. Try to be taking the picture from the top or from below. By doing that, you can have different perspectives of the scene.

6. Always look for candid shots.

Looking for candid shots can actually provide you with more opportunities of taking the best shots. When you check out different photos, you will find that some of the best ones are those that are taken without the subjects looking at the camera. Capture scenes where people are doing their usual things, and you will see how natural it would become.

7. Make use of UV filters on the front of your camera lenses.

UV filters can provide your camera with the protection that it needs, in order to stay in top condition. Place the filters in front of your camera lenses, so that your lenses would be protected from scrapes or knocks. With that, you can be assured that your lenses last longer.

8. Buy different lenses and swap with a fellow photography enthusiast to save money.

Camera lenses are quite expensive these days; and, having a good number of them would offer you more when it comes to taking pictures. However, if you want to save on cost, then find a friend who has the same brand of camera that you have. Aside from that, have an agreement with him in purchasing different lenses, so that you can simply swap lenses whenever you need to.

9. Use a remote if you still get blurred shots even with the use of a tripod.

Even with the use of a tripod, there is still a possibility that you would get blurred shots. This can be due to the way you press the shutter button, in taking the pictures. To get around that, all you actually need to have is a remote. Aside from that, you can also make use of your camera's delay timer.

10. Make use of your mobile phone's camera if you are trying to scope for beautiful landscape shots. So you won't forget them.

Scoping for great landscape shots can become a fun activity, especially if you won't keep on forgetting those that you want to visit later on. To prevent that from keep on happening, you can always make use of your mobile phone's camera for it. By doing that, you would be able to remember where you want to shoot your landscape scene next, by simply checking your phone.

11. How to make sure that your lenses would not knock against each other while being put inside your bag.

Camera lenses do not come very cheap these days, which is why you need to take care of them properly. To make sure that they won't destroy each other while being put inside the bag though, you can use your hiking socks for them. All you have to do is to cut the shocks into its proper sizes. Just make sure that the socks are cleaned so that your lens would not get dirt on it.

12. Provide yourself some time to look through the photographs that you have taken a while ago.

Checking out your work after a few weeks that you have taken them, can provide you a new feeling for the photos. Aside from that, it would also give you the opportunity to see what you did right, and what you did wrong. More importantly, even if you did really well with them, you can always use them as your guide to make improvements.

13. How to take pictures of fast moving or unpredictable subjects.

There are times when you want to capture an image or images of subjects that are erratic or moving fast. An example of this would be your pet dog playing around the garden. To make sure that you can capture a decent picture, simply make use of your camera's continuous shooting mode. With that, it would take a number of shots in just a second, which would give you the chance to catch a good shot.

14. What you can do to become a wedding photographer.

If you want to become a wedding photographer, you want to start it right, so that you can get more clients. Staring out right in photography means gathering more information about it.

However, you should also practice more; and, one of the best ways to do that is to volunteer as one of the photographers for your friend's or relative's wedding celebration.

15. How to make sure that you are buying the right kind of lens, especially if it expensive.

Lenses are available in different models these days. Some are big, while some are small. Keep in mind that such camera accessories are quite pricey. To make sure that you would be purchasing the right kind though, you can always rent certain types of lens for a few days first, so that you can check out their many functions and advantages, which should help you make the right purchase.

16. Create a homemade light box if you are trying to take pictures of your products.

If you are trying to sell certain products online and you want to take pictures of them, you should have a good light box for it, so that your pictures would really look good. A homemade light box can be made with a cardboard box and a tracing paper. With your homemade light box, you can take quality pictures of the products, which would help in selling them faster.

17. Lower down your camera.

In most cases, you would usually take a picture standing up. Try lowering it down for certain types of shots, so that you can also explore different angles. Checking out different perspectives would provide you with more options on how you want to go about in taking a picture of your subject. Aside from that, lowering down your camera is one of the best things to do when your subject is small.

18. Make your hobby pay you for all your hard work.

To gain more motivation in taking beautiful pictures, one of the best things that you can do with them is to sell them on stock photography websites. These sites can expose your pictures to people who are looking for the best images for their marketing efforts. In other words, if companies find that your pictures are in good quality, and they are applicable to their products, then they would purchase it.

19. Use plastic LCD screen protectors.

You need to protect your camera's LCD screen at all times, since it is where you would check the images you captured. To achieve that, you can simply make use of LCD screen protectors for them. They can ensure that your LCD would be free from scratches and dirt. Thus, with them, you can maintain the quality of your digital camera for a longer period of time.

20. Manipulate light.

Capturing light for the picture that you are taking is considered by some as an art. To manipulate light, you need to consider the different sources of it, such as the sun, flashes, and lamps. You have to know that these different sources may also need different tools, in order to take advantage of them, such as the reflectors, diffusers, and snoots.

21. Check out the exif data.

When you check back on your pictures, it is best to check out the camera settings when you took them. Some of the setting you want to know about regarding this would include the aperture, shutter speed, and such. To do that, refer to the exif data of the pictures. By doing that, it can help you take note of the things you have done right or you have done wrong, and make improvements.

22. Use your flash outdoors.

This idea may seem a bit funny for some. However, using your flash when you are taking pictures outside is actually a good idea. It is often referred to by professionals as "fill flash". Using your flash outside can help light up your subject even on a sunny day, especially if the light is coming from behind them.

23. How to take pictures of sunsets.

Setting your white balance to daylight and not to auto is a good idea when taking pictures of sunrises or sunsets. Oftentimes, when there is lower amount of light, your camera may not provide you the best photo for it. Thus, it is best to set it to daylight, or better yet, put the white balance mode to manual.

24. Back up your images.

Backing up your images is one of the most important things you need to do. You can easily do it by purchasing an external hard drive for your computer. By backing up your images, you are assured that they won't get lost. Back up your photos every one or two weeks, and store the it in a place that is safe.

25. How to manage your hard drive space.

Managing your hard drive space is very important, since it is where you would store your images. Save space on your hard drive by spending some time in sorting out the images. Select the images that you really want to keep. After doing that, all those that you have not selected should be deleted, so that you can save more room for future photos.

26. Reason to avoid the built in flash.

In using the built in flash of your camera, it can provide an undesirable effect to your subject. It can leave your subject with too much light. Thus, if you can save up some money, it is best to invest on a quality external flash. Pair it with a diffuser, and learn how to make use of them properly to obtain the best photo quality.

27. Talk to your subjects.

When you are trying to take portraits, it is best to talk to your subjects while you are doing it. When you talk to them, it would make them more comfortable in front of the camera, which makes the photos look more natural. Aside from that, it can also provide you a chance to take candid shots.

28. Testing out the modes of your camera.

If you have just bought a brand new camera, one of the first things that you can do is to test out its different modes. You should try out its auto mode, manual mode, and such. By doing that, you would become more familiar of its settings. Thus, you would learn more about what settings to use in different types of photo taking.

29. What to do without using a tripod.

If you don't have a tripod, you can still take quality photos by bracing yourself while shooting. You can do this by leaning against a wall, or resting your camera on top of a stable object. Aside from that though, to make sure that the photos are not blurred, it is best to hold your breath when pressing the on the shutter button.

30. Always return the settings of your camera to the average one.

There are times when you want to take pictures while you are strolling around the park, or at your neighborhood. To make sure that you can take an instant shot, it is best that you always put your camera on regular settings. With that, you would be able to snap on it immediately, without having to go through lots of hassles in getting the right settings.

31. Doing a trick with sunglasses.

Increasing the color saturation can still be done even with the use of a compact camera. All you have to do is to hold your sunglasses on top of the lens, in which it would serve as its polarizing filter. This would reduce the glare and reflections. However, take a few shots first, so that you can ensure that you won't include the frames of your sunglasses into the picture.

32. Do some experimenting.

Lots of beginners in photography are pretty serious in following all the things they learned through the books they read. To stand out from the rest, you should do some experimenting by not sticking to the rules all the time. When you do that, you would be able to discover new techniques and compare different perspectives.

33. Have your own calling cards.

Having your own calling cards is a good way to let people know that you can offer your photography services to them. However, it is also one of the things you can do to make sure that you won't be offending someone, when you take their picture off the street. If someone confronts you, just hand over the card, so that he would realize that you are an artist or a professional. By doing that, the person would feel good that you have chosen him as your subject.

34. How to decide in deleting or keeping the image.

Oftentimes, you might find yourself out of space to save your photos in. Therefore, it is best to decide on what images to keep and what images to delete. To decide on deleting an image, just simply think about hanging it on your wall. If you don't like the thought of doing that, then that means that the image should be deleted.

35. Build your portfolio.

Whether you want to become a professional photographer or not, building a portfolio can still offer lots of advantages. Building one can be done online, in which all you have to do is to save your best photographs in a certain website, after signing up for your own account. By doing that, you would be able to check your photos easily, even when you are away from home, and set your standards higher.

36. Making sure that the photo tells a story.

Prior to hitting the shutter in taking a picture, it is best to take some time to check your subject, as well as the frame. Try to see if the subject blends well with its background, and other things that would be included in the photo. By doing that, you would be able to ensure that your photograph would tell a story.

37. Setting yourself up for a challenge.

Improving your creativity can be done by challenging yourself in taking at least one good photograph each day. Even if you don't feel like it, you need to stand up, and take a picture even for the most uninspiring objects. By doing that, you would later on realize that you can simply make use of your imagination, in order to take interesting pictures.

38. Read the user manual.

Many people today do not take time in reading the user manual of their digital cameras, assuming that all of the functions can be learned by simply playing with them. However, if you try to sit down and give it some time, you would realize that there are things that you can really learn from it. Reading your user manual would provide you a way to learn more about your camera's functionality.

39. Shooting pictures in the city.

Taking pictures in the city can be dull for some people. However, there are actually lots of ways that you can make the pictures look more interesting. One of which is to go to a multi-story parking lot, and take pictures at its different levels. By doing that, you would be able see great views of the city. Aside from that, it would also offer a fresh perspective over the usual ground shots.

40. Don't let rain get you affected.

Oftentimes, when it is raining, you could find yourself getting discouraged in taking pictures. However, there are actually lots of ways that you can go around it, and still take beautiful images. For example, taking a picture through a window that is covered with rain would provide you a gloomy effect for a change.

41. What to use as a light reflector.

Having a light reflector can help you a lot when it comes to taking portraits. Using a large piece of paper that is colored in white can already be used as your light reflector. With a white paper reflector, you can use it for portraits, as well as for still-lifes. Do some experimentation, so that you can achieve the kind of quality you want.

42. How to prevent your subject closing his eyes.

If you usually end up with pictures of kids closing their eyes when they blink at the wrong moment, you can actually do a simple trick to prevent it from happening again. You can simply tell him to close his eyes, and open them only when you would say so. Tell him to smile as well, so that you would be able to take a good portrait picture, in which has his eyes opened and he is smiling.

43. A trick to get your focus right.

Oftentimes, people find it quite difficult to get the focus right in doing a self portrait. To get around it, you can turn off the lights, while holding a flash light just right next to your eye. While you are doing that, press your remote shutter half way down to trigger its auto focus. After which, just turn the lights back on and take your self portrait. Your camera should already have the right focus by then.

44. Using a compact camera.

Using a compact camera can produce images that are not in top quality if it is not set in optical zoom. With that, it is best if you know how to recognize or change it from digital to optical zoom. To achieve that, you can always check the user's manual that comes with it.

45. Taking pictures while traveling.

When you are traveling, one of the best ways to learn more about the best spots to take pictures at, is to check out brochures about it. Aside from that, you can also visit travel blogs and sites.

By doing these things, you can take a glimpse of marvelous landscape pictures, which should give you a better idea about where to situate yourself when you reach your destination.

46. Not having the right exposure?

It can be tricky to get the right exposure at times with a new camera. To fix it, you can always put it in Auto mode and take a snap at an object. It the picture comes out in good quality, then check out the settings that the camera has chosen for it. With that, take note of the settings, so that you can follow it in the future.

47. Don't forget to visit the website of your camera's manufacturer.

Do not forget to visit the web portal of the company that made your digital camera. In most cases, when there are new software or firmware updates, it would be posted on the site, and you can download it easily. Aside from that, you can also take advantage of its section, where people and technical persons would discuss certain issues.

48. Presets.

One of the best things about modern digital cameras these days, is the fact that they can allow you to have your own presets. With presets, you can identify the settings that you deem most appropriate for certain scenes. Save your presets, so that you can easily activate them when needed.

49. Taking care of your camera's batteries.

Camera batteries need proper care in order for them to last longer. One of the best things that you can do for it is to let it get drained once or twice in a month. Once it is fully discharge though, make sure that you also charge it properly. This practice would ensure that you are extending the life of your batteries.

50. What to do with spots on the pictures.

There are times when you may see certain spots on your pictures. When this happens, it could be a sign that your lens or sensor has dust on it. Try to blow it and take another picture. However, if you want to make sure not to experience it again, you should purchase a cleaning kit for your sensor soon.

51. How to properly take pictures of fireworks.

Fireworks can be quite tricky to capture. However, there are certain steps that you can take to take beautiful photos of them. A couple of them would be to make use of a tripod, and make sure that your focus is set to its maximum level. Aside from that, use longer shutter speeds for it around a one second to five seconds.

52. Shooting a moving object.

If you want to take pictures of a moving object, then make sure that your camera is equipped with an auto focus tracking mode, or something similar to it. This feature will make your camera to track the moving object automatically, while constantly adjusting its focus. With that, all you have to do is to make sure that you are going to get the composition right.

53. Try to enjoy your hobby.

If you want to become good in photography, you should learn to enjoy it. Don't be too hard on yourself, whenever you come up with shots that are not satisfactory. Getting no decent shots can actually happen even to the best photographers. When that happens, challenge yourself and practice more.

54. Using natural reflectors.

Using natural reflectors can bring out the best in your photographs. For example, if you are shooting pictures at the beach, the white sand can serve as your giant reflector. To take advantage of it, have your subject sit down on the sand. Aside from the sand, water can also serve as a good reflector.

55. Shooting pictures on a cloudy day.

If you want to take excellent portraits outdoors, then do it on a cloudy day. When it is cloudy, it would actually even out the light. This is due to the fact that the clouds can serve as your giant reflector. Aside from that, it can also control the light coming from the sun, which can allow you to take full advantage of your flash.

56. Using a broom handle instead of a light stand.

If you have an assistant with you when you are taking portraits, it is a good idea to place the flash at the end of a broom stick. Let your assistant hold it at the proper point. By doing this, you won't have to worry about the stand getting knocked over due to the strong winds. This can help you work faster, and with more convenience.

57. Try to come up with three photos in a row.

When shooting pictures of children, you should try to take three or more photos in a row. This way, you would be able to capture their movements, which can become quite funny or interesting. After taking the photos, you can simply put them all in a film strip, which you can do with a software program. The pictures when presented well should tell a story about the kids.

58. Don't let your model wait for you.

Having a model wait for you is not a good way to start. This can make him or her lose that energy, which you would need in coming up with beautiful portraits. Thus, before your model arrives at your place, you should do your preparations beforehand. Have it done hours before, so that you can start immediately minutes after your model would show up.

59. Pay attention to the background.

Keep in mind that the subject of your photo should be the one that would capture the attention of the people viewing it. Therefore, you should be mindful of the background. With a background that can distract a viewer's attention, your subject's smile or pose may be neglected. Thus, choose the background well, so that the focus would remain on the subject of your photo.

60. Don't delete photos while inside the camera.

While the pictures are still inside the camera, it is not wise to delete them yet, especially if you are unsure. This is because the LCD screen may not provide you with the right way to judge the shot, due to the fact that it is not big enough. Therefore, it is best to transfer the photos to your computer first, before selecting the ones that you want to delete.

61. How to have perfect candid shots.

Candid shots that are took in the perfect moment would help you achieve what you want to portray. It is quite challenging though, but one way to do it perfectly would be to predict the next movement or action of your subject. For example, if you want to portray the faces of the members of a soccer team after winning the game, then take pictures of them just when the competition is about to end.

62. Shooting group portraits.

To bring out the best in a group portrait, try not to have their heads in a straight line. In other words, try to vary the heights of their heads so that the picture would become more natural and interesting. For example, if you are taking a family picture outside, situate them near a group of large boulders, so that they would sit on different levels.

63. Spacing in group portraits.

When the right spacing is observed, a group portrait would look more beautiful. Although people would want to have more space in between them when they pose for a group picture, it is still better to put them closer together. Try to explain this to them, so that they would be able to understand.

64. Know your subject better.

When someone hires you to take pictures for his or her event, it is wise to get to know them better. By knowing your client, you would know what sort of pictures he would and would not like. When you are able to learn more about your subject, you would have more chances of taking pictures that would reflect your client's personality.

65. Shooting subjects with long noses.

When your subject has a long nose, it can become a distraction once the photo is taken. To make sure that this is not the case, what you can do is to shoot the subject head on. Aside from that, it would also be wise to have his chin slightly up. In doing it this way, the person viewing the photo would not even notice the long nose.

66. Know your camera well.

It is always best that you know how to set your camera properly, in accordance to its surroundings. However, this may not be enough, since you may be asked by your client to take pictures in different places in the venue, which requires different effects. Thus, apart from knowing the settings of your gear, you should also have the ability to switch them quickly.

67. Check out the poses before taking the shot.

Before taking pictures of your model, try to use your imagination when it comes to the poses you want him or her to do. Aside from that, you should also think of ways of how your model can do it. Once you have thought of the poses, let your model execute them the way you want it to be done, and try out some new things.

68. How to minimize reflections from glasses.

When you shoot subjects that wear glasses, there is a possibility of glare on the glasses. Having glare on the glasses is not a good sight to see. To get around it though, all you need to do is to invest on a good polarizer. When you put on the polarizer, it would greatly solve your problem.

69. Don't be too reliant on your DSLR.

It is true that having a DSLR would provide you better picture quality than your point and shoot gear. However, it is not a good reason to miss out on a great moment that is worth capturing, just because you were not able to bring it with you. If you feel that a moment that you should capture is about to unfold, you should click away with whatever you have.

70. Don't forget to come up with a list.

When you are about to leave your place to perform a shoot, it is always better to have a list of what you need to bring. Aside from the things to bring, the list should also indicate certain processes you need to do prior to leaving. Some of which would include charging the batteries, testing your camera, transferring the pictures to your PC to empty your memory card, and so on.

71. Shoot with other photographers.

It is always best to shoot with other photographers, especially with those that are more experienced than you are. This way, you get to learn lots of things from them, such as their techniques, their equipment, their style, and a lot more. Aside from that, you can also make new friends. Doing this would certainly offer you an opportunity to learn lots of new things.

72. Think first and slow down.

There are times when it is better to slow down taking pictures and think. This would provide you a way to listen to yourself. By doing that, you can come up with brighter ideas, better poses, better angles, and a lot more. Thus, before you press on your shutter, try to think about the image you are capturing first.

73. How not to forget client's name.

You could become quite uncomfortable when you are talking with a client, while taking his pictures, and you forgot his name. One of the ways to prevent that is to write down his name on a sticky note, and let it stick at the back of your camera. Make sure to make the note small enough for him not to notice it.

74. Taking a picture of a person with deep set eyes.

When you take portraits, you may eventually come across a client who has deep set eyes. When you take his picture, you would realize that it can cause deep shadows to appear on his eyes. To get around that, all you actually have to do is to lower your source of light a little. By doing that, you can ensure that the light can reach the space under his brow.

75. Hiding wrinkles.

If your client has wrinkles and you want to impress him by coming up with pictures that do not show them, then what you can do is to use a larger type of light source. This can make the pictures soft, especially if you bring the light closer. Aside from that, you can also use more frontal light, instead of side light.

76. Choosing a model.

Choosing a model should be done carefully, especially if you are trying to come up with pictures for a commercial. In most cases, people would prefer ladies who look really hot. However, you should also make sure that you are choosing someone who is approachable and friendly. By doing this, you can ensure that you would be able to work with her easily.

77. Take pictures.

If you consider yourself as a beginner in this field, you should not be afraid in taking more and more pictures. You can now purchase a memory card that can provide you with lots of space for your pictures. Thus, you should shoot as many times as possible, for the more times you do it, the better it would be for you when it comes to learning.

78. Emphasize your subject.

When you take a picture, you should emphasize your subject as much as possible. When you check the frame, your subject should not appear small in it. Make use of your camera's zoom, or move closer to the subject, so that you can fill the frame with her. When you do that, you should also try to come up with ways to emphasize her desirable features.

79. Preview your shots.

To ensure that you have the right exposure in taking the shots, you should learn how to preview them properly. When you are taking pictures under the bright sun, it can become tricky because of the light. Thus, you should find shade, so that you would be able to see it clearly.

80. Don't focus too much on the mega pixels.

When you listen to people in trying to shop for digital cameras, you could often hear them asking about the mega pixels of the products, and would even go for those with larger ones. You should not focus too much on this, since larger mega pixels simple means it gives you a way to print pictures larger without affecting their quality. Unless you are selling poster sized prints, you won't have to get the camera with the largest mega pixels.

81. Spare battery.

It is always best to carry a number of extra batteries on your bag when you are shooting pictures. This is because, you would never know when a great moment could happen; and, running out on battery juice can make you miss it. Charge all your extra batteries and bring them, so that you won't have to miss out on great shots.

82. Learn more tricks from others.

Learning is something that you need to do when it comes to photography, even if you have been with it for a number of years. Thus, it is always best to be open about new techniques, new methods, and such. Keep in mind that even the best photographers learn from each other; thus, it is also best for you if you do so.

83. Take a photography course.

As a beginner in photography, you need to find ways to learn more about it. One of which is to take a photography course right at your own place. By going through a course, you would be able to gather more information about the subject. Aside from that, you may even be taught about certain techniques that other beginners did not have the benefit to learn about.

84. Try shooting black and white.

You should always do something different from time to time, so that you can come up with more interesting shots. One example of it is to shoot pictures in black and white. One of the things that you can observe with black and white shots is that, they are usually very interesting, even if you thought they would be boring.

85. Try capturing the subject off center.

When you take pictures, you would probably put your subject at the middle of the frame. However, if you check out professionally taken photos, most of them are actually made more interesting, since their subjects are captured away from the center of the frame. Therefore, try to picture your subject off center, and see the big difference.

86. Carry your camera with you.

If you don't want to miss out on great photo opportunities, then make sure to carry your camera with you at all times. This means to bring it with you while riding the bus, strolling at the park, walking around the neighborhood, and such. If you do this, you would be amazed of the number of photos you have taken that are really breathtaking.

87. Find your theme.

There are times when you need to be inspired, in order to have that drive to take beautiful pictures. However, you can also boost your motivation by coming up with a theme that you like. Some of the themes that are quite popular today would include playing kids, different weather conditions, playing dogs, and many more.

88. Consider what's behind your subject.

In taking pictures of a subject, you should not forget considering what is behind him. Your backdrop should be something that would not distract the viewer of the photograph. Aside from that, it should also become part of the whole picture or image, which can help tell a story about the place or subject.

89. Shoot the subject in their own environment.

There are times when your subject becomes uncomfortable in being at your studio; and, this can show in the pictures. Thus, it is best that you shoot the subject at his own place. For example, instead of letting your clients bring their child with them at your studio, visit them at their place. Let the child be at his playpen, and you would definitely capture lots of interesting images of him.

90. Consider the height of your subject.

When you shoot pictures of subjects who are smaller than you are, then you should not take pictures of them at your usual standing point. You should get down on the ground, and capture moments at the same level as they are. This is applicable in taking pictures of small children. Aside from that, you should also take note of this, when taking pictures of small animals like dogs.

91. Using window light.

If you don't have a studio at your own place yet, and you want to make use of natural light in taking pictures of your subject, don't forget that your window can help you out with it. When light from outside passes through a glass window, it actually becomes diffused. Thus, you can simply have your subject position himself right next to it, so as to take advantage of the light.

92. Try taking a picture of something smaller.

When you want to diversify, try to take pictures of something smaller. This could include the hands of a child, the feet of your spouse, and such. Keep in mind that there are lots of small things in this world that are beautiful, which are worth capturing. Just keep an open eye for them, so that you would be able to find them.

93. Waving.

When you are trying to take family pictures, one of the things that can happen, which can ruin a good one would be lots of waving. This is true, especially when there are lots of members in the family. Thus, it is best to let them settle down first. Aside from that, you can also gently inform them to stop the waving just for a few moments, since their hands may cover other members' faces.

94. Considering how your photo is going to be used for.

To make your client more satisfied with your photograph, you should consider what the photos are going to be used for. This is because it would help you determine better on what sort of style you want to use. For example, if you re taking a picture of a couple to announce their wedding, then it is best to do it horizontally, since it can provide more space on the side for their names or for their message.

95. Don't face the sun.

Letting your subject face the sun for a midday post is actually not a good idea, since it can create shadows on her face. For a midday shoot, it is best to let her face away from the sun, in which her face would be in the shade. To make sure that her face is exposed properly, over expose the picture to achieve that effect.

96. Use a prop.

Considering the comfort of your model would take you a long way as far as taking quality pictures is concerned. Thus, if you see that your model is getting a bit uncomfortable, what you can do is to give her a prop, such as a toy, a flower, or any kind of small object she can hold on to. Doing that would make her feel comfortable. Aside from that, the prop could even add more spice in the photo, although you don't have to include it in the frame.

97. Make it more interesting.

Interesting pictures would surely grab lots of people's attention. One of the things that you can do to achieve that is to become more creative on how you position your subject. Examples would include having a woman looking through a window, placing a child inside the crib, and so on.

98. Try different lightings.

Trying both high key and low key lightings is a good idea. This is because there are some persons who would actually look better in the pictures when they are overexposed, while others are the complete opposites. Thus, it is best to explore further when it comes to lighting, so that you can achieve the kind of feel you want for your photos.

99. Research about your camera before making the purchase.

Before you purchase a digital camera for your newfound hobby, you should do your research about it first. Researching can be done through the internet, in which all you have to do is to visit the website of the manufacturers, in order to gather more details. Aside from that, you can also check out reviews, to learn about the experiences of people in using the camera in question.

100.   Ask a professional photographer for feedback.

If you are a beginner, and you have a friend who knows a professional photographer, try to see if you can meet him. If you can, then take advantage of the moment, and ask him for feedback on your photos. By doing that, you would be able to make improvements on your skills, by listening to his advice. Aside from that, he could even become your mentor.

101.   Learn from others online.

Learning more about photography can actually be done online these days. There are lots of web portals that are launched for it. Aside from that, there are also online forums, which are usually visited by both beginners and professionals in the field. With that, it can provide you an opportunity to ask them questions about different things regarding photography.

Printed by Libri Plureos GmbH in Hamburg, Germany